Mainz

City and Cathedral Guide

by Michael Imhof and Simone Kestin

Monument for the Romans in Mainz-Kastel, 1990. The inscription says: "Romans of the XIIII. legion founded Castellum Mattiacorum from which today's citadel results.")

History

Mogontiacum – Roman Foundations

above right: replica of a Roman ship in Löhrstrasse, where it was discovered (the original is kept in the museum for ancient seafaring)

Around 13–12 BC, Drusus, the stepson of Augustus Caesar (27 BC – 14 AD), established a camp for two legions, each of 6,000 men, to act as the base for the planned conquest of the territories to the east of the Rhine. A settlement grew up around the camp called 'Moguntia', named after the Celtic god Mogon. This settlement became the capital of the new province of Germania Superior (Upper Germania), not least due to the construction in 27 AD of a bridge over the Rhine with a fortified bridgehead (in what is now Mainz-Kastel). As well as the legionaries' barracks, the military base included a central administrative building, a shrine for the legions' standards and a spa with a steam bath. A supply of water was provided by an aqueduct that opened out into the camp.

The civilian town attached itself to the camp, hemmed in by the military stores on the Weisenau and the notional harbour at the so-called 'Dimesser Ort', today's container port. The largest public building was the theatre. This stood at the settlement's southern exit and could accommodate an audience of 10,000. During excavation works for the 'Römerpassage' (Roman Passage) shopping centre, the foundations of a shrine to Isis and the Mater Magna were also uncovered.

Roman Mainz was frequently the victim of invasions by the Teutons. After the fall of the limes, the fortified frontier, established in the 1st century, the previously scattered settlements were therefore brought together and surrounded by a wall. However, under Emperor Valentinian by the end of the 4th century at the latest, the

Jupiter's column on Deutschhausplatz (the original is in the national museum). It was erected in honour of emperor Nero between 54 and 68 AD by merchants and craftsmen besides the road leading from the Roman camp to the harbour.

camp was abandoned following countless invasions by the Alemanni. In 406/7, the Vandals, Sueves and Burgundians finally managed to take the town completely.

Mainz in the Early Middle Ages

Although Roman Mainz no longer existed, some of the structures of the ancient town remained. These related largely to the administration of Christianity, which was the official state religion since the 4th century. The first recorded mention of a Bishop of Mainz goes back to the year 346. Despite the unrest caused by the Germanic tribes' conquest, Christianity remained one of the town's decisive and controlling factors. From around 500 AD, Christianity became firmly established again and countless churches were built. Of these, however, the only trace that remains today is at St. Alban's church. Briefly interrupted, the list of bishops began again around 565 with Sidonius, the 'Restorer of the destroyed houses of God'.

"Roman stones" above Untere Zahlbacher Strasse and south of the St.-Hildegardis-Hospital respectively (about 1.4 km south-east of the main station). There are 57 remains of pillars once belonging to an eight kilometres long aqueduct which was built in 69–79 AD. It once consisted of presumably 500 pillars which were up to 35 m high and carried water from the springs near Drais and Finthen across the Zahlbachtal to the citadel of Mainz.

The Apostle of the Germans and first Archbishop of Mainz, Boniface (747–754), received the Archbishop's mitre from the Pope in 747, and this became firmly tied to Mainz during the term of his successor Lullus

right:
Copperplate engraving by Matthäus Merian, 1646. It shows early modern Mainz with its medieval town wall, the church of St. Stephan, the cathedral and the Liebfrauenkirche, as well as the Martinsburg (to the right).

Sign on the church of St. John (detail). In 2004 the Boniface route was inaugurated. It is a hiking path that follows the route taken to convey the body of Boniface from Mainz to Fulda in 754.

Market portal of the cathedral (detail)

(754–786). A little later, Charlemagne reinstated the metropolitan constitution, which had been introduced back in Roman times but had lapsed in the interim. This meant bringing together several bishoprics into one ecclesiastical province with an archbishop as metropolitan at its head. As a result, under Bishop Lullus – Boniface's pupil and successor – Mainz became the largest ecclesiastical province in Christendom, with 15 suffragan bishoprics from Verden an der Aller to Chur and Prague.

Archbishop Liutbert (863–89) restored the Roman city walls as protection from the Normans, and under Archbishop Hatto I (891–913) a new cathedral was built, the nave walls of which are largely retained in today's Johanniskirche (St. John's Church).

The most dominant personality of the latter part of the 10th century was Archbishop Willigis (975–1011). He had an enormous cathedral built that even then had the dimensions of the current cathedral, and from which the towers on the eastern side of the chancel and the foundations remain. Willigis was advisor to three kings, and administrator of the Empire while Otto III was yet to come of age. In 975 he secured from the Pope the right to crown the Holy Roman Emperor, and in 1002, subsequently presided over the coronation of Henry II. Archbishop Willigis was simultaneously Archchancellor of the German Empire and the highest ranking of the seven Electors. Under him, there was such a build up of power in Mainz that even in the 11th century contemporary historians were extolling the city as a 'golden capital of all cities', as 'Aurea Moguntia'.

As far back as the early 10th century, Jews involved in trading far and wide settled in the city, soon becoming one of the largest Jewish communities in the West. The devastating pogrom of 1096 cost some 600–700 Jews their lives. Their houses were in the area between Betzelgasse (Betzel Lane) and Flachsmarkt (Flax Market), where Jews lived again in the 13th and 14th centuries.

In the 11th century, the townsfolk, who were gaining in strength, turned away from the archbishops and took the side of Emperor Henry IV in the

Oldest Monument to Gutenberg by Joseph Scholl, today situated in the gateway of the Gutenberg Museum

Investiture Dispute. When they again subordinated themselves to the power of the Church, represented by Archbishop Adalbert I (1111–37), they were rewarded around 1119 with a privilege that included the first rights of self-administration. A few years later, the city's fortifications were partially destroyed and the ban of the Empire was imposed over Mainz.

Middle Ages and Renaissance

From the 13th to 15th century, Mainz was a blossoming free city of the Empire. In 1244, the people obtained the right to free council elections and, in 1254, they took over government with Speyer and Worms in the Federation of Rhineland Cities. The first recorded reference to a town hall dates from 1277. In the second half of the 13th century, the wealthy townsfolk had numerous parish churches and monasteries built, with various different orders settling in the city, including Carmelites, Franciscans and Antonites.

The city's reputation was also enhanced by Johannes Gutenberg (c. 1398–1468), the inventor of the printing press with movable letters.

In 1462, however, after the feud between Archbishop Adolf II of Nassau (1461–75) and Archbishop Diether II of Isenburg (1475–82), Mainz lost its political power and all of its privileges. This meant the end of self-administration by the people and economic plight. Even the founding of the university in 1477 could not rescue the city's tarnished reputation. After Archbishop Diether of Isenburg had the Martinsburg castle built in 1478–81, thus relocating the archbishop's residence from the cathedral to the northwest edge of the town, Mainz became henceforth a princely and flourishing archiepiscopal capital.

That changed for a while as a result of the Reformation. The wealth of the church suffered through the loss of income from the archdiocese, in which the territorial princes gave their backing to the Reformation. Still worse was the pillage by Margrave Albrecht Alcibiades von Brandenburg-Kulmbach (1522–57), the mercenary leader of the prince's party, which was

above right and left: Former barracks in the shape of a horseshoe, 1833. Situated on the banks of the river Rhine in Mainz-Kastel the building houses today the Museum Castellum which exhibits Roman relics and models of bridges crossing the Rhine.

below: Theodor-Heuss-Bridge, built in 1882–85 by Friedrich von Thiersch. After the Roman bridge and a wooden bridge built by Charles the Great, it was the first massive bridge crossing the Rhine.

opposed to the emperor and thus aligned with France. Despite being paid, he had churches, monasteries and curiae destroyed, as well as all the chapter houses outside the walls.

In the course of the Counter Reformation at the end of the 16th century, increasing influence was exerted by the Jesuits, who had moved into what until then had been the Minorite monastery in 1577 (building the 'Domus Universitatis' in 1615–17).

Renewed Upturn after the Thirty Years War

During the war, Mainz was occupied by the French and the Swedish until the Peace of Westphalia in 1648. Afterwards, Elector Johann Philipp von Schönborn (1647–73) reinforced the medieval city walls with modern fortifications, moved the Altmünster convent and St. Petersstift into the city and established the Bleichenviertel district in 1663 to compensate for the torn down districts on the outskirts. The city was taken by the French without a battle in the Palatinate War of Succession (1688/89). Building works (including the summer residence 'Favorite', destroyed in 1792/93) began again under Elector and Bishop of Bamberg, Lothar Franz von Schönborn (1695–1729). Elector Johann Friedrich Carl von Ostein (1743–63) completed the Electoral palace in 1752 with the addition of the north wing, while Emmerich Joseph von Breidbach-Bürresheim (1763–74) erected the new Electoral stables on the 'Große Bleiche' avenue. This was followed by the building of new churches (St. Peter's, St. Ignatius, the Augustinian and the Jesuit church) and of countless noble houses. After the Jesuits were turned out, the university was reformed under Elector Friedrich Karl Josef von Erthal (1774–1802). The charterhouse and the Reichklaren and Altmünster convents were converted into university buildings.

Mainz in the 19th and 20th Century

In 1792, French revolutionary troops occupied the city. When it was retaken by the Imperial army in 1793, many of the most significant buildings suffered severe damage and several, being in ruins, disappeared completely a short time later. These included the Liebfrauenkirche (Church of our Lady), the Jesuitenkirche (Jesuit Church), St. Gangolf, Martinsburg castle and Schloss Favorite. From 1797–1814 Mainz once again became French. After their withdrawal, Mainz and the outlying areas of Kastel and Kostheim were annexed to the Grand Duchy of

Hessen. The German Federation now held sway over the city, and under it new building projects were gradually developed, including construction of the city's theatre and repairs of the cathedral. After losing the university in 1816/17, Mainz finally became no more than a provincial town. However, the size of the population was showing the opposite trend, with the figure for 1809 doubling to 47,731 residents by 1871.

The Mainz carnival, one of the most famous carnivals in Germany, was established in the first half of the 19th century, with the Mainzer Ranzengarde (Mainz Knapsack Guard) formed in 1837 and the Mainzer Carneval-Verein (Mainz Carnival Society) in 1838. The construction of the new town from 1872, erection of the Rhine Bridge (1880–85) and laying of the railway by the city's master builder Eduard Kreyßig stimulated building progress. The splendid Kaiserstrasse was created as a dividing line with the old town, culminating with the Christuskirche (Christchurch). In 1884, the main railway station was moved to its current location, and when the inner, customs harbour was opened in 1887, Mainz was able to regain a little of its earlier importance.

At the beginning of the 20th century, the city walls were opened up and the first incorporations of neighbouring areas began, starting with Mombach. The districts in the north served as new industrial sites, while in the southwest a villa quarter was built to plans by Friedrich Pützer.

The Second World War destroyed the major part of the old town in Mainz, with heavy bombing raids in 1942 and 1945. In 1946, approval was given to re-establish the university, and in 1950 Mainz was made the capital of the Federal State of Rhineland Palatinate, formed four years earlier.

Rebuilding work moved at a slow pace. Even up to 1965, countless ruins were still being torn down. It was not until Ernst May was put in charge of city planning that an effective transport and building strategy was drawn up for the old town.

In 1962, Mainz became the home of the Zweites Deutsches Fernsehen – ZDF (the second of Germany's two national state broadcasters). The company made its base in the new district of Lerchenberg. To this day, Mainz remains an important location for media of all kinds, as well as other flourishing companies, whose modern buildings complement the city's historic appearance.

above and below: New monuments to carnival on Schillerplatz

below: Mainz seen from the river Rhine

The Cathedral of SS. Martin and Stephan

History of the Building

Statue of St. Boniface in front of the Chapel of St. Gotthard in the cathedral (Copy. The original was made by Kaspar Hiernle in 1750 and is kept in the Cathedral Museum).

right:
Eastern choir of the Cathedral seen from Liebfrauenplatz

Along with the cathedrals at Worms and Speyer, Mainz cathedral is one of the three Imperial cathedrals of the Rhine. Its function as the old empire's main church and the site of seven royal coronations, plus its role as the cathedral of the archbishops of Mainz, gave it a great importance.

It is highly likely that Mainz became a diocesan town in the 3rd century, even though a bishop of Mainz is first mentioned in 346. From 560, there is a fully sequential bishops' roll, and in 747 holy Boniface, Apostle of the Germans, became the city's first archbishop, holding the position until his murder in 754.

The first early Christian cathedral district from the time of Emperor Constantine († 337) was under the western part of today's cathedral and below the Johanniskirche (St. John's Church) to the west, which is possibly the former bishop's church from the time around 900.

Cathedral area in the 13th/14th century

Immediately after his appointment by Emperor Otto II in 975, the determined Archbishop Willigis (975–1011) began with the construction of a great new cathedral. However, one day before it was due to be consecrated in 1009, the cathedral burnt to the ground, which is why, when he died, Willigis had to be laid to rest in St. Stephan's. The two staircase towers of the original building and parts of the old west transept have, however, survived. The layout of the Ottonian building continued to play a decisive role when the cathedral was rebuilt, as the new structure, consecrated in 1036 under Archbishop Bardo (1031–51), was erected on the old foundations.

However, after a fire in 1081, changes began to be made to the Ottonian/early Salinian cathedral, which was gradually replaced with a more ornate, Romanesque structure. As a result of the fire, it was decided to renew the nave and the east chancel. Building work dragged on until 1137, with the Bardo crypt not finished until 1872– 1876. Instead of a flat wooden roof, as was still customary at that time, the nave was given a vaulted stone ceiling. Next to Speyer Cathedral, this makes Mainz Cathedral the oldest stone vaulted building in Germany. At the same time, around 1130, Archbishop Adalbert I of Saarbrücken (1111–37) had the Gotthardkapelle (Gotthard Chapel) built as a chapel for the court and palace. A further phase of building began under Archbishop Konrad I. of Wittelsbach (1183–1200). However, these works were not completed and consecrated until 1239 under Archbishop Siegfried III of Eppstein (1230–49). The work done in this phase included the construction in 1210 of the 'Memorie', plus renewal of the external walls of the aisle and of the west side of the building with a clover-leaf design in the style of

Page 11: Cloister, crossing tower and western transept

South portal at the eastern transept

below: Market portal with the bronze doors from Willigis' cathedral of 988

Cologne Cathedral. From 1279, further extensions were added in the form of Gothic chantry chapels.

In 1418, Archbishop Johann II of Nassau (1397–1419) established a double chapel in the eastern part of the central nave, parts of which still remain. Between 1480 and 1490, the Romanesque west tower was made higher with the addition of a late Gothic belfry, and shortly afterwards, prior to 1498, the Marienkapelle (Chapel of St. Mary) was integrated.

The fires of 1767 and 1793 had a significant bearing on how the building subsequently took shape. In 1771, engineering captain Franz Ignaz Michael Neumann (1733–85), son of Würzburg master builder Balthasar Neumann, erected a stone Baroque crown on the tower above its Gothic tier. Between 1769 and 1774 the towers adjacent to the west chancel also got new Baroque crowns, and an image of holy Martin with the beggar (copy) was added to the ridge of the roof.

The dissolution of the Archbishop's office in 1798 was followed by the deconsecration of the cathedral, with furnishings and large parts of the cathedral's treasures being lost. The building itself was just saved from being torn down by Bishop Joseph Ludwig Colmar (1802–18), installed in 1802 by Napoleon. As a result, it was possible to return it to its original destiny as early as 1804. In 1813/14, the sacred building was again temporarily used for other purposes, serving the Napoleonic troops as a military hospital, barracks and stables.

In 1828, the east tower, which had been increased in height in 1361, was given an egg-shape iron cupola made to plans by Georg Moller, senior building officer of the state of Hesse-Darmstadt. However, as it was in danger of collapsing, the cupola and the entire tower structure had to be taken down and rebuilt from 1870–79 by Petrus Cuypers (1827–1921). Before the New Romanesque building we see today was completed, the side stair towers in the upper floors and the east crypt were reconstructed to the original plans of Henry IV.

The cathedral was largely spared by the Second World War. However, the roof, with the exception of the stone west chancel, was gutted by fire. Repairs to this wartime damage and some internal conversions were made from 1955–60. When the exterior was renovated from 1971–75, the cathedral was given its brownish red coating, which lends a homogeneity to the design and helps to harmonise the different phases of construction.

Mainz cathedral is one of the coronation churches of the old Empire, in which the coronations of seven Emperors took place. The cathedral today faces the open 'Liebfrauenplatz' (Square of our Lady) to the east and is surrounded by the former chantry buildings to the south and by shops and residential property to the north and west. Its dimensions are as follows: External length, 113m; internal length, 109m; length of the central nave, 53m; width of the central aisle, 13.5m; height of the apex of the central nave vaulting, 29m; internal height of the east cupola, 38m; internal height of the west cupola, 44m; height of the west tower, 82.5m; height of the east staircase tower, 55.5m.

The Interior

The oldest sculptural decoration consists of the bronze Willigis wings of the market portal door (the main portal). According to the inscription these were cast by master craftsman Berenger for Archbishop Willigis in 988. After the bronze doors of Aachen Cathedral that Charlemagne had fitted, these door wings are the oldest remaining in Germany. The freedom privileges given to the people of Mainz in 1119 by Archbishop Adalbert of Saarbrücken were set into the doorframe inlays in 1135. The portal framing and the tympanum with its representation of the enthroned Christ come from the time around 1200.
The interior impresses visitors with its great size and imposing, raised double chancel complex (i.e. a chancel both in the east and the west) combined with a crossing cupola.

Interior of the cathedral: View into the eastern choir (11th century). The pulpit was renovated in a neogothic manner in 1834 by J. Scholl.

Mainz, cathedral,
ground plan
(after Winterfeld)

red = c. 1009
green = c. 1100–25
blue = c. 1137
yellow = 1190–1239
violet = gothic

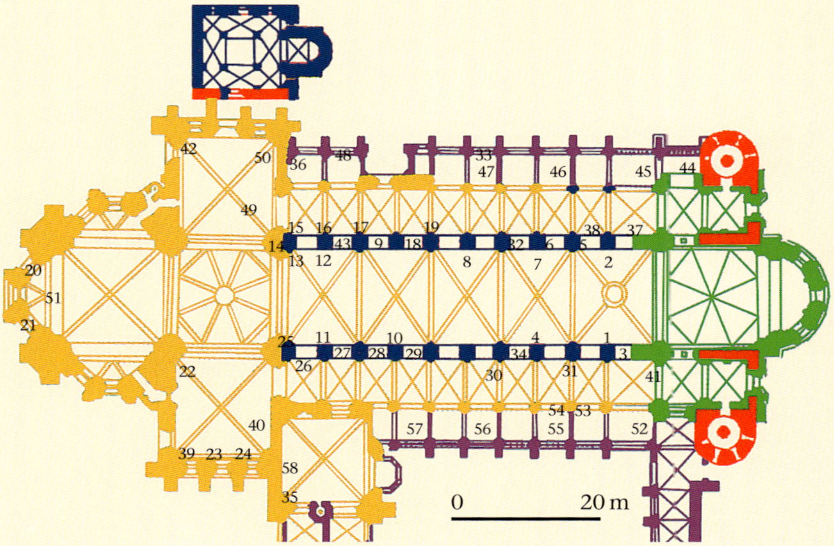

Monuments to archbishops

1 Siegfried II. von Eppstein († 1249).
2 Peter von Aspelt († 1320).
3 Mathias von Bucheck († 1328).
4 Adolf I. von Nassau († 1390).
5 Konrad III., Rhein- und Wildgraf von Daun († c. 1434) by Madern Gerthener.
6 St. Boniface († 754), 1357 (formerly in the church of St. John).
7 Johann II. von Nassau († 1419); probably a work by Madern Gerthener.
8 Diether von Isenburg († 1482); statues of Catherine and Barbara (right), Martin and Boniface (left).
9 Lothar Franz von Metternich-Borschedt (Burscheid; † 1675).
10 Berthold von Henneberg († 1504), by Hans Backoffen.
11 Jakob von Liebenstein († 1508), by Hans Backoffen.
12 Uriel von Gemmingen († 1514), by Hans Backoffen.
13 Johann Adam von Bicken († 1604).
14 Albrecht von Brandenburg († 1545).
15 Albrecht von Brandenburg († 1545), by Dietrich Schro.
16 Sebastian von Heusenstamm († 1555), by Dietrich Schro 1559.
17 Brendel von Homberg († 1582) supposedly by Nikolaus Dickhart.
18 Wolfgang von Dalberg († 1601).
19 Wolfgang von Dalberg († 1601) from 1606.
20 Johann Philipp von Schönborn († 1673)
21 Lothar Franz von Schönborn († 1729)
22 Konrad II. von Weinsperg († 1396).
23 Johann Friedrich Carl von Ostein († 1763), by Heinrich Jung from Hochheim.
24 Philipp Carl von Eltz-Kempenich († 1743) by Burkhard Zamels, 1740.
25 Berthold von Henneberg († 1504).
26 Georg Friedrich von Greiffenklau († 1629).
27 Damian Hartard von der Leyen († 1678).
28 Carl Heinrich von Metternich zu Beilstein und Winneburg († 1679).
29 Anselm Kasimir von Wambold († 1647).
30 Damian Hartard von der Leyen († 1678) by Arnold Harnisch.
31 Anselm Franz von Ingelheim († 1695), 1703–1711, maybe by J. W. Frölicher

Other monuments

32 Bishop Johann Jakob Humann († 1834), made by the sculptor J. Scholl of Mainz in 1836.
33 Bishop Frh. Wilhelm Emmanuel von Ketteler († 1877), in the chapel of St. Mary (outer wall of the cathedral).
34 Bishop Josef Ludwig Colmar († 1818), by Josef Scholl, 1834.
35 Electoral councillor Martin von Heusenstamm († 1550), 1553.
36 Administrator Adalbert von Sachsen († 1484, aged only twenty); monumental main figure by the so-called "Adalbertmeister", side figures probably by Hans von Düren.
37 Karl Adam von Lamberg († 1689), ascribed to J. W. Frölicher from Frankfurt.
38 Provost Christian Rudolf von Stadion († 1700) and Johann Philipp von Stadion († 1742).
39 Provost Carl Emmerich Franz von Breidbach-Bürresheim († 1743), by Johann Peter Melchior between 1763 and 1770.
40 Provost Heinrich Ferdinand von der Leyen zu Nickenich († 1714), by J. M. Gröninger.
41 Georg Christian von Hessen († 1677), by Arnold Harnisch.
42 Dean Bernhard von Breidenbach (Traveller to Palestine, † 1497)
43 Provost Johann Wilhelm Wolf Metternich zur Gracht († 1694).

Altars and statues

44 Altar of Jodocus von Riedt, 1622.
45 St. Mary's altar in the chapel of St. Barbara; donated between 1652 and 1668; crucifix by Matthias Rauchmüller (about 1657).
46 "Bassenheimer Altar" in the St. Magnus chapel; built in 1610, in front of the altar an Entombment of Christ of late gothic times (about 1495; formerly in the Liebfrauenkirche), work by the "Adalbertmeister".
47 winged altarpiece in the chapel of St. Mary (1875); late gothic figures Boniface, Mary and Martin (c. 1515).
48 lay altar in the chapel of the sacrament, about 1657.
49 baptismal font, 1328.
50 "Nassauer Altar", shortly after 1601.
51 Rococo choir stalls by Franz Anton Hermann, 1760–67.
52 "Scharfenstein-Altar" in the All Saints' Chapel, 1609.
53 Christ and Thomas, 1521, school of Hans Backoffen.
54 St. Denis, about 1410
55 St. John's altar, about 1620.
56 St. Laurentiusaltar, donated in 1676.
57 St. Michael's altar, 1662.
58 Bishop's seat, composed of stones with Roman inscriptions.

Page 15: Interior of the cathedral. View into the western choir.

The central nave, with its narrow arcades of pillars and three-level separation, looks steep and tall, while in the blind arches of the clerestory there are murals of the life of Jesus painted by the Nazarene artist Philipp Veit (1793–1877) and his pupils, dating from 1859–64.

The late Romanesque west building has a grand and monumental appearance with rich and varied external decoration. It consists of a high transept, octagonal, monumental crossing tower, a raised chancel with three apses and two adjacent towers. A choir screen created by the 'Naumburg Master' in 1239 originally closed off the altar room. Today, sections of the figures are on display in the cathedral museum. The screen was replaced in 1682 with the early Baroque chancel platforms. The main altar, put in place in 1960, stands in the centre of the west chancel. A simple bronze crucifix hangs above it. This was created by Georg Zeuner from Speyer to celebrate the cathedral's 1000th anniversary in 1975. The cathedra crowned by the holy Martin stands in the centre of the horseshoe-shaped choir stalls. The stalls, made of dark oak, were carved by Franz Anton Hermann, court carpenter in Mainz from 1760–67. The glass windows made by A. Wendling were created in 1954 to a design by H. Leitermann of Mainz. They show the coats of arms of all of the bishops of Mainz, over 90 in total. The Lullus crypt built in 1928 below the west chancel serves as the burial site of the bishops of Mainz.

The east chancel (St. Stephan's) has survived from Salian times (11th century). The Bardo crypt, extended between 1872–76 and accessible from the side, is located below the raised chancel complex with its new Romanesque ciborium altar. On the altar in the crypt is a relic shrine created in 1960 by Mainz goldsmith Richard Weiland. The shrine contains the relics of 22 revered holy men and women from the bishopric of Mainz.

The Gotthardkapelle (Gotthard Chapel) adjoins the northern side of the west transept. It is a central, two-storey building that used to be crowned by a tower. Archbishop Adalbert of Saarbrücken had it built in 1137 as an episcopal chapel and as his own chapel of rest and palace chapel. Shortly after Adalbert's death in 1137, it was consecrated under the patronage of the holy Godehard (Gotthard). The chapel was adjoined by the first episcopal court prior to the construction of the Martinsburg castle in 1481. The red, yellow and blue paintwork dating from 1985 reflects the way it looked during the Staufer era. The interior is dominated by a large, wooden Romanesque crucifix from Udenheim (c. 1140) with parts of the original framework and an octagonal bronze candlestick made by G. G. Zeuner in 1971. A wide opening links the two floors, on which the bishop above and his following below used to listen to mass together.

Following Boniface († 754), 84 archbishops ruled in Mainz, of whom 45 are buried in the cathedral. The cathedral therefore contains a remarkable number of medieval and early modern burial monuments. Leading through artistic eras from Gothic to Classicism, these allow an almost complete sequence of archbishops and bishops to be reconstructed from Siegfried III († 1249) to Bishop von Ketteler († 1874).

Until 1390, the monuments were constructed as tombs. When the room to do this within the cathedral was all used up, epitaphs were created instead (e.g. the monument to Konrad von Weinsberg, † 1394), with the body laid to rest nearby under a more simple

Gotthard-Chapel with the crucifix of Udenheim (about 1150). The chapel was consecrated to St. Godehard in 1137 and originally served as a private chapel for the archbischops.

Monument to St. Boniface († 754) from 1357 (originally kept in the church of St. John)

slab. Since Gothic times, monuments were usually crowned with a baldachin, and until the Baroque era the deceased was portrayed in an idealised pose with pallium and bishop's crook. The outstanding works in the cathedral include mural monuments created by Hans Backoffen for archbishops Berthold von Henneberg († 1504), Jakob von Liebenstein († 1508) and Uriel von Gemmingen († 1514).

Two new types of monument appeared in the 16th century. The Renaissance monument with aedicula frames (e.g. the monument to Albrecht von Brandenburg, d. 1545, ascribed to Dietrich Schro) and the family epitaph (e.g. the monument to Daniel Brendel von Homburg). In the 17th century, rigid architectural framing gave way to scenes of three-dimensional figures. Examples of these are the epitaphs in the west chancel created between 1738–45 by Johann Wolfgang von Auvera for archbishops Johann Philipp († 1673) and Lothar Franz von Schönborn († 1729). The grand Rococo style of monument is represented by the epitaph in the west transept created by Burkhard Zamels for Elector Philipp Karl von Eltz († 1743). The largest monument in the cathedral is 8.33m high and 4.73m wide. It is the monument to the cathedral dean Heinrich Ferdinand von der Leyen zu Nickenich († 1714), erected in the west transept and commissioned by the dean himself prior to his death.

Many of the cathedral's former furnishings no longer exist. These include winged altars made by Mathias Grünewald (1475–1528). However, in the north side aisle, built along with several chantry chapels from 1279, a number of artefacts remain, including the altar of the holy Victor (1622), the Magnus altar (1610–13) and the Barbara altar (1657). Adjacent to the chapels on the south side, the visitor can also still see the Scharfenstein altar of 1609 in the Allerheiligenkapelle (All Saints' Chapel), the St. Johannesaltar (St. John's Altar) from c. 1620 and the Michaelsaltar of 1662.

The new Gothic Marienaltar (St. Mary's altar) in the Marienkapelle (Chapel of St. Mary) built in 1495 also conceals a further treasure. A sculpture created around 1510–20 of the 'Schönen Maria von Mainz' (Beautiful St. Mary of Mainz) accompanied by the Saints Martin and Boniface, from the school of court sculpture Hans Backoffen. The chapel also serves as the last resting place of the beneficent Bishop von Kettler (d. 1877).

Other items of historical and artistic note include a late Gothic burial stone (c. 1495, a work of Adalbert's master craftsman) from the former Liebfrauenkirche (Church of our Lady). The St. Magnus Chapel also contains an octagonal baptismal font in the north of the west transept. The font, made of tin, was cast in 1328 by Johannes the master craftsman. It also originates from the Liebfrauenkirche and shows figures in Gothic blind tracery including Christ, Saint Martin and Mary and the apostles. The Nassau altar next to it was probably created in 1601 by Johann Jakob Juncker.

The 'Fastradas' burial stone from St. Alban is thought to be in memory of Charlemagne's third wife, who was buried in Mainz in 794. This area is adjoined by the so-called 'Memorie', built in the 13th century. This was used at one time as a chapter house and later as the canons' chapel of memory to the dead. Its truncated apse was replaced in 1486 by a small Aegidian chancel. Inside the Memorie there is a stone prelate's seat and several epitaphs, including those of Nikolaus Dickhart and Dietrich Schro. The

Monument to archbishop Diether von Isenburg († 1482) with St. Martin and St. Boniface

Inner courtyard of the cloister and west end of the cathedral

Gothic entrance portal, called the 'Memorial Portal' and dating from c. 1420, was artistically designed by master cathedral builder Madern Gerthener of Frankfurt. The portal figures are high quality examples of the so-called 'Weicher Stil' (soft style). Saint Martin is portrayed in the tympanum of the adjacent Romanesque portal (early 13th century), which had already been walled up by 1425.

The cloister

The cloister, with two floors and three wings, stretches along the south side of the cathedral. It was built under Madern Gerthener's direction between 1397–1410 to replace its Romanesque predecessor. The cathedral library used to be on the cloister's upper floor. The burial stones on the first floor of the east wing include that of Heinrich von Meißen, a minstrel also known as 'Frauenlob' (Praise the Ladies), who died in 1318. In the past, the canons lived in the annexed chantry buildings (chapter houses) to the south, which today accommodate the cathedral and diocesan museum.

The tympanum portrayal on the graveyard portal (the so-called 'Paradiespforte' or 'Galilee porch', 1210–20) on the south transept depicts Christ on the throne as judge of the world, surrounded by John, Mary and two bishops.

Cathedral and Diocesan Museum

The episcopal cathedral and diocesan museum was opened in 1925 and contains many valuable sacral works of art formerly kept in Mainz cathedral and other churches of the bishopric. It is housed in the area around the cathedral cloister, including the former chapter room. The outstanding works in the museum include the Hatto window from St. Mauritius (c. 900), a Carolingian priest's stone (9th century), early Gothic reliefs from the cathedral's former west choir screen

(c. 1239), which rank among the most famous sculptures from the Naumburg Master, and a Madonna from the Fuststrasse (c. 1250).

The cathedral treasury has a number of particularly valuable items of liturgical equipment on display. The majority of these are the work of silversmiths and goldsmiths and include: Monstrances; mass chalices (including the 'Brautbecher' or Bride's Cup, thought to be French, dating from around 1330); relic chests; bishop's crooks; crosses; book covers; and valuable tapestries.

Johanniskirche (St. John's Church)

Originally consecrated to Saint Martin, the Johanniskirche was probably the city's first cathedral church and is the oldest sacral building in Mainz. The body of St. Boniface was therefore probably laid out in the Roman building that preceded it prior to being transported to Fulda following his martyrdom in Dokkum, near Groningen in the Netherlands. Archbishop Hatto I (893–913) had the current building constructed around the year 900. After the consecration of the new cathedral, with which it was linked through the galilee porch demolished in the 18th century, this three-aisled basilica received the patronage of St. John the Baptist as a collegiate church. The west chancel was added around 1320–25 in place of the west apse. After dissolution of the chapter in 1802, St. John's served as a protestant parish church, with both the east apse, which had been pulled down in 1737/38, and the east façade being rebuilt. After being gutted by fire in 1942, the church was restored to its

St. John's Church, west choir, 1320–25

Cathedral and Diocesan Museum: opening hours Tue–Fri 10 a.m.– 5 p.m., Sat & Sun 11 a.m.– 6 p.m. closed on mondays and high days

www.dommuseum-mainz.de

left: Cathedral and Diocesan Museum, fragment "The Damned" of the former western rood screen, The Naumburg Master, about 1239

St. John's Church, c. 900 and 1320–25, view into the choir

St. John's Church, view from south east

Romanesque condition ten years later under the direction of Karl Gruber from Darmstadt. There is a Gothic portal on the south transept with a figure of Saint George in the tympanum. The portal originates from the cathedral deanery's St. Georgen-Kapelle (Chapel of St. George), which was demolished in 1829. The figure of Saint John on the south side of the nave was created in 1906 for the then main portal by Carlo Culot to a design by Augusto Varnesi.

Leichhof (Graveyard)

This square to the south of the cathedral still bears the name of the cathedral graveyard, which ceased to be used in the 12th century at the latest. Until the 18th century this former 'Gerümpelmarkt' (junk market) was characterised by its row of market stalls, and until the cathedral fire of 1767 was enclosed on the north side by the so-called 'Paradies' (galilee porch) between the cathedral and the Johanniskirche. To replace the buildings destroyed by the fire in 1775, Franz Ignaz Michael Neumann (1733–85) designed cathedral chapter houses at numbers 26–36 Leichof and 2–4 Schöfferstrasse, which were built from 1778–79.

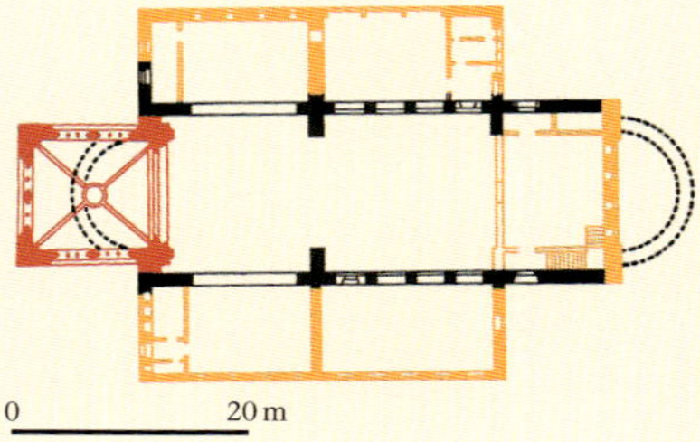

St. John's Church, ground plan
black = c. 900
red = c. 1320–25
orange = mainly 1952

right: This stair tower stands between Gutenberg square and market. It was built in the first half of the 17th century and is crowned by a figure of St. Barbara (1717).

Marktplatz (Market Square)

The market square is bordered to the south by the cathedral and to the north by rows of houses extending towards the north east of the town. The houses were destroyed in the Second World War, but have since been faithfully rebuilt. Only the cathedral houses built in front of the cathedral in 1771 to plans by Johann Valentin Thomann are still original.

Rising to 6.4m in the centre of the market square is the 'Heunensäule' column, which originates from the Bullau hills near Miltenberg am Main. It is said to have been intended for Mainz cathedral in the year 1000, but was never used. The people of Miltenberg ultimately gave it to the City of Mainz in 1975 for the cathedral's anniversary. A bronze cuff at the foot of the column designed by Gernot Rumpf recalls historic events in the city with inscriptions and ornate symbols (e.g. emperors' crowns and bishops' mitres).

The market square fountain is the oldest Renaissance fountain in Germany. It was installed in 1526 under Elector Albrecht von Brandenburg (1514–45) to commemorate victory in Emperor Charles V's battle at Pavia and the end of the Peasants' War. Above the entablature with the benefactor's inscription, cherubs hold the coat of arms of the benefactor and – since restoration in 1767 – that of Elector Emmerich

"Leichhof" (Graveyard) square and the west tower of the cathedral in the background

Market square with the Heunensäule

The Heunensäule, c. 1000 AD and 1980

below: The market fountain, 1526

Liebfrauenkirche, engraving from around 1800

above right: Former prussian main guard (Haus am Dom)

Joseph von Breidbach-Bürresheim (1763–74). The fountain is crowned by the Saints Martin, Boniface and Ulrich and carries on top a Madonna, added when Valentin Barth renovated the fountain in 1890.

Liebfrauenplatz (Square of our Lady)

To the east, the Liebfrauenplatz abuts the cathedral's east façade. The 'Square of our Lady' is named after the former church of the same name, a stately Gothic collegiate church that was connected by an atrium to the cathedral's east building. The church was founded in 975, converted in the 11th century and renewed in Gothic style around 1410. During the French occupation of 1793, the church was badly damaged and was torn down in 1807. The dimensions of the church can now be seen once again thanks to the reconstructed foundations. Items of the high quality medieval church furnishings are today exhibited in the cathedral and the 'Landesmuseum' (State Museum).

Liebfrauenplatz is bordered to the south by the former main Prussian sentry house dating from 1829 (*Haus am Dom*, No. 8 Liebfrauenplatz). Reduced in length in 1966 and changed into a porch-style building, this used to be the site of the 'Liebfrauenkirche' cloister.

House "Zum römischen Kaiser"(Gutenberg Museum), 1653–64

In 1916, the 'Nagelsäule' (Column of Nails) was erected on the Liebfrauenplatz. It was designed by Adolf Gelius and made by the sculptor Ludwig Lipp. The centre of the war memorial column forms a bundle of nailed oak trunks with carved reliefs and inscriptions, crowned by an iron cross.

Gutenberg-Museum

(No. 5 Liebfrauenplatz)

The administrative offices of the Gutenberg Museum and the 'Zentrum der Gutenberg-Forschung' (Gutenberg Research Centre) are housed in the 'Haus zum Römischen Kaiser' (The Roman Emperor). Destroyed in 1945 and then rebuilt, this three-storey building was originally erected between 1653–64 for the Electoral council and the master bursar Edmund Rokoch. Domenco Rosso's decorative stucco ceiling, with a wealth of figures, dating from the time the building was first constructed were retained in the entrance driveway. The stairwell also has its stucco decorations. From 1742, the

Column of Nails, 1916.

House "Zum römischen Kaiser" (Gutenberg Museum), stucco ceiling in the gateway by Domenico Rosso, c. 1665

The Solms-Laubach copy is one of the Gutenberg bibles with 42 lines that have been printed between 1452 and 1455

Stair tower (1584) from the former "Schöfferhof" (No. 22/24 Schusterstrasse) which was owned by a printer named Schöffer in the 15th century

Gutenberg Museum opening hours:
Tue–Sat 9 a.m.–5 p.m.,
Sun 11 a.m.–5 p.m.
www.gutenberg-museum.de

building served as a prestigious hotel, in which Goethe, Mozart, Voltaire and others stayed. The sculpture of Emperor Charles VI above the portal originates from this period. The rear buildings, with two courtyard complexes, were not rebuilt following their destruction in 1945.

The 1960's building that houses the exhibition rooms of the Gutenberg Museum was modernised in the year 2000 and linked by a steel and glass bridge to the new extension built by the architects Rossmann & Partners. The Museum was established by the people of Mainz in 1900 to mark the 500th birthday of Johannes Gutenberg (1397–1468). The museum's treasures include historic prints, graphics, printing presses, print-setting machines and ornate medieval manuscripts. These include the 'Apocalypse', a blockbook printed around 1463 using wooden tablets, the 'Mainz Psalter' of 1493, the 'Schedelsche Weltchronik' (Schedel's Chronicle of the World also known as The Nuremberg Chronicle) also of 1493 and 'Theuerdank' from 1517. The museum's prized possessions also naturally include the 42-line Gutenberg Bible.

Gutenberg Museum, printing workshop

Heilig-Geist-Spital (Hospital of the Holy Spirit)

(No. 2 Rentengasse)

The Hospital of the Holy Spirit is the oldest intact burghers' hospital in Germany. It was built from 1236 on replacing a cathedral chapter hospital first mentioned in 1145. Municipally controlled since 1244, it served as an old people's home for women from the 15th century, had numerous functions in the 19th century, and has been an inn since 1863. Forfeiting part of the building's authentic substance, it was reconstructed in 1975 to what is presumed to be its original late Romanesque condition. Since 1862, the east portal has been in the north transept of the cathedral and was replaced by a copy. Of the original patients' ward inside the building, three aisles of the hall, with its pillars and cross vaulted ceiling, have been retained. Above this lies the former chapel that protrudes on the façade with its bay-like apse. Shortly after 1462, the hospital ceased to use the single-storey ward in the northern part of the building in favour of today's two-storey Gothic room.

Hof zum Korb, No. 6 Am Brand, 15th cent.

Hof zum Korb (Wicker House)

(No. 6 Am Brand)

Until its destruction in 1945, the district to the north of the market with its once narrow lanes 'Am Brand' and 'Korbgasse' (Wicker Lane) formed the oldest area of merchants' housing in Mainz, made up of Romanesque and Gothic houses. However, the town hall from the 13th century and the general store built in 1317 were demolished already in the 19th century. All that remained, once tightly enclosed by buildings, was the late medieval, 15th century 'Haus zum Korb' (Wicker House), that Gutenberg's successor, Peter Schöffer, united with the Gutenberg printing works in 1476 along with the adjoining 'Hof zum Humbrecht' (Humbrecht House). The Madonna (c. 1350) below the small corner tower is now a cast, as is the Holy Blood Madonna (c. 1420) on the general store corner of Korbgasse. The spiral staircase tower (1584) of the former Schöfferhof (Schöffer House) is also very nearby.

above: Heilig-Geist-Spital (Hospital of the Holy Spirit), c. 1236 and 1462.

Rathaus (Town Hall)

The town hall was built between 1971–73 by the Danish Architect Arne Jacobsen. Standing on a triangular site with an inner courtyard, it still looks imposing today, while the rhythmically scaled structure of its façade makes it an interesting building. The Town Hall Square is connected to the pedestrian zone by a large bridge.

below: The town hall, 1971–73.

Eisenturm (Iron Tower)

The six-storey iron tower is named after the Eisenmarkt (iron market) that was held on the bank of the Rhine. Flanked by two adjoining structures, it was erected in 1240 and made taller in the first half of the 15th century. After it had lost its purpose at the end of the 16th century, it was quickly surrounded by houses. In the 18th century, the tower was used as a prison. Today it serves as a studio and exhibition space. The gateway of the tower facing the Rhine is designed as a grand portico with depictions of lions. On the east side the visitor can still make out the connection to the former city wall with its gangway.

left and below: Iron Tower, c. 1240 and first half of the 15th century.

No. 75 Augustinerstrasse, 1st half of the 17th century

Leichhofstrasse/Kirschgarten (Graveyard Road / Cherry Garden)

The best preserved and most picturesque quarter of the Mainz old town is formed by the area around Leichhofstrasse, Kirschgarten, Heiliggrabgasse, Schönbornstrasse, Augustinerstrasse and Kartäuserstrasse. The roads are characterised by attractive old buildings, such as the 'Haus zum Spiegel' (Mirror House) at no. 1 Leichhofstrasse, a half-timbered early 17th century house with oriel. The houses in Kirschgarten are particularly old, originating mainly from the 15th to 18th centuries. The half-timbered houses at no. 16 (end of the 16th century), nos. 26–28 (end of the 15th century) and no. 30 (first half of the 16th century) are especially noteworthy. The fountain dates from 1932, the column is crowned by a copy of the Harxheim Madonna. The square is named after the spring "Kirschbornquelle" that comes up at the Rochusspital (Rochus Hospital).

No. 1 Leichhofstrasse, Mirror House, end of 17th century

No. 26/28 Kirschgarten, Haus zum Aschaffenburg, c. 1500, and No. 19 Kirschgarten, Haus zum Beimburg, end of 16th century

left: No. 23 Kirschgarten (17th cent.), No. 25 (18th cent.), No. 27 (20th cent.) and No. 29 (1760/70)

below: Fountain in Kirschgarten, 1932

Augustinian Church, 1768–72, and Augustinian Monastery, 1737–53

right: Augustinian Church, façade with the crowning of Mary (copy from 1859)

Augustinerkirche und -kloster (Augustinian Church and Monastery)

(No. 34 and 40 Augustinerstrasse)

The Augustinians built their first church in Mainz in 1260–87. This was replaced by today's hall church, built to a design by stonemason Georg Schrantz. In 1805, it became the 'Bischöfliche Seminarkirche' (Episcopal Seminary Church), and in 1851, after a murder was committed in the church, it was reconsecrated.

The church is enclosed by buildings on three sides. On its façade above the portal is a depiction of the crowning of Mary (a copy from 1859), flanked by the Saints Augustine and Monica, with the Holy Trinity above on a throne. In 1772, the painter Johann Baptist Enderle portrayed the baptism and glorification of Saint Augustine in what is now the only originally preserved ceiling mural in any of Mainz's Baroque or Rococo churches. The split organ with its central window was made by Johann Heinrich Stumm in 1773 and now ranks as one of Europe's most significant late Baroque organs. Displayed in an alcove of the church is an image of a Mother of God Enthroned, created around 1420 and rescued from the burning Liebfrauenkirche in 1793.

In the course of secularisation, the abbey was dissolved in 1802. Since 1805, the Augustinians' monastery buildings dating from 1737–53 have been used as priest's seminaries. The mo-

Augustinian Church, 1768–72, interior with stucco decoration by Andreas Henkel and ceiling frescoes by Joh. Bap. Enderle, 1772.

left:
Augustinian Church, enthroned Madonna, c. 1420

right:
Portal of the Augustinian monastery showing a statue of Mary accompanied by two Augustinian saints. The sculptures were made by Niklolaus Binterim in 1753

No. 7 Heringsbrunnengasse, baroque burgher's house with oriel and a relief depicting the Lamentation of Christ (c. 1710)

nastery's doorway is particularly grand, with sculptures by Nikolaus Binterim of 'Maria von der Tröstung' (Mary of the Solace) flanked by two Augustinian saints. The chronogram dated 1753 refers to the time of the monastery's origin, while the buildings include the well preserved library of 1639 with its ceiling murals, the refectory with a stucco ceiling and the stairwell, completed in 1749.

Erbacher Hof (Erbach House)

(No. 9 Himmelsgasse)

Himmelsgasse (Heaven's Lane) is the location of the city residence of the Cistercian monastery at Eberbach im Rheingau. Now the diocese of Mainz training centre, the buildings were first mentioned in 1777 and damaged in the Second World War. The angular building to the north of the site and the perimeter walls of the south wing with its unusually large, groin vaulted cellar complex, still come in part from the 12th century. The central building, constructed around 1250, incorporates the Marienkapelle (Chapel of St. Mary) the earliest Gothic building in Mainz. It is painted with scenes from the lives of Christ and Mary, plus portrayals from the Old Testament.

Johanniterkommende (Hospitallers' Commandery)

(No. 2 Heiliggrabgasse)

This stately Baroque palace of the former commandery of the Hospitallers of the Holy Sepulchre (since 1969 the 'Bischöfliches Ordinariat', Bishop's Palace) was built between 1740–48 to

Hospitallers' Commandery, No. 2 Heiliggrabgasse, 1740–48.

below left and middle: Erbach House, Chapel of St. Mary, c. 1250

Monument to bishop von Ketteler by Thomas Duttenhöfer (1993) on Bischofsplatz.

plans drawn up by the German Order's master builder Johann Caspar Bagnato (1696–1757) and revisions made by Anselm Franz von Ritter zu Grünstein. It was built on a medieval forerunner, remnants from the chapel of which remained intact and were only demolished in 1960. In the interior several high quality stucco ceilings have been preserved.

Since 1993, there has been a monument to the 'Socially aware bishop', Wilhelm Emmanuel Freiherr von Ketteler (1850–77), created by Thomas Duttenhöfer, on the nearby Bischofsplatz (Bishop's Square), named after the former Bishop's Palace.

Weihergarten (Pond Garden)

The houses built on the Weihergarten are considered to be outstanding examples of classicist residential architecture in Mainz as the 18th century drew to a close. Architect Emanuel Joseph von Herigoyen (1746–1817) designed the three curiae (nos. 10, 11 and 12) in 1790 in the early classicist style. The music publishers, Schott, who have existed in Mainz for over 225 years, had their company offices in number 5, dating from 1793. In the inner courtyard of that very house, where Wagner was reciting the text of the 'Meistersinger' as far back as 1862, serenade concerts still occasionally take place.

Holzturm (Wooden Tower)

Erected in the first half of the 15th century, this six-storey gate tower stands at the point where the old town meets the outlying district of Selenhofen, enclosed within the city walls in the 13th century. Named after a wood store, the tower served as a city gate and from time to time as a prison. Colourful busts of two couples, one of merchant stock one royal, are depicted on the first floor windows on the city side. In the gate's embrasure, now lying some 3 metres lower, high water marks form reminders of the floods of 1565, 1573 and 1784.

Haus zum Stein (Stonehouse)

(No. 1 Weintorstrasse)

Built at the end of the 12th century, this three-storey Romanesque residential tower is the oldest remaining secu-

above and left: Wooden Tower, first half of the 15th cent.

No. 12 and 10 Weihergarten, both 1790–91

Stonehouse, No. 1 Weintorstrasse, end of the 12th century

St. Ignatius, 1763–75, façade (below left), interior with high altar (p. 35), copy of a crucifixion group after Hans Backoffen, 1519 (the original is kept in the Cathedral Museum, right) and one side altar (below right)

lar building in Mainz and a rare example of preserved Romanesque towers of this type. In 1981–83, the tower was renovated and partially restored to its Romanesque state

St. Ignaz (St. Ignatius Church)

(No. 40 Kapuzinerstrasse)

After the medieval parish church was pulled down, a new church and garden were built between 1763–75 to plans drawn up by the court stucco plasterer of Electoral Mainz, Johann Peter Jäger, who also oversaw the construction. The cross-shaped hall church is consecrated to Ignatius, the martyr and Bishop of Antioch. Its vaulted ceiling was built by Johann Valentin Thomann (1695–1777). A

sculpture of St. Ignatius, a Last Supper relief (both made in 1772 by Johann Jakob Junker) and four alcove figures by Nikolaus Binterim (until 1790 in the Carthusian monastery in Mainz) adorn the 30-metre high west façade. From 1764–73 a crypt was subsequently built into the church. This now contains 198 burial niche graves one on top of the other of benefactors, builders and artists, including Hans Backoffen and his wife. The ceiling mural in the interior of the church was produced in 1773–74 by Johann Baptist Enderle. Overpainted in 1902 by Waldemar Kolmsperger and restored in 1953–55, it depicts scenes from the life of the church's patron. The early classicist side altar was created in 1774–80 by Johann Peter Metz, while the freestanding baldachin altar was completed in 1784.

In the garden there is a copy (the original is in the cathedral museum) of a crucifixion group begun by Hans Backoffen and completed by his pupils. The inscription indicates that this was donated by the sculptor and his wife in 1519.

Museum for ancient seafaring, view into the exhibition hall with original and reconstructed Roman ships

Museum für antike Schiffahrt (Museum of Ancient Seafaring)

(No. 2B Neutorstrasse)

Founded in 1994, this museum displays items from research into 'ancient seafaring' undertaken by the Römisch-Germanisches Zentralmuseum in Mainz. Unique in Germany, the exhibits include five original shipwrecks from Late Antiquity and a fully reconstructed model ship. These remains of the City of Mainz Rhine fleet were found during excavation work in 1981/82 around 7.5m below current street level. The location of the find, right outside the former Roman city wall, was probably part of the earlier harbour.

The museum's role is the academic study of Roman seafaring, drawing on all sources, presenting and reconstructing its history. Models of ships in 1:10 scale are therefore also exhibited, while blueprints, geographical charts and views of the historic surroundings complete the varied presentation.

The exhibition is housed in the former central workshop for locomotive repairs, built shortly before 1880.

Zitadelle (Citadel)

To the south-west of the city centre lies the Jakobsberg hill and the citadel. The Benedictine abbey of St. Jacob was built on the hill in 1050. From 1620–26, Elector Johann Schweickardt von Kronberg had a dry moat built around it, and in 1659–61 Elector Johann Philipp von Schönborn had a new right-angled structure built on the site with four corner bastions. The three-winged command post building was erected in 1696 under Elector Franz Lothar von Schönborn, and restored to its original condition in 1950 after being badly damaged in the War. Two allegorical sandstone figures have survived on the front of the main building. These were created by Johann Sebasti-

Museum für antike Schiffahrt opening hours: Tue–Sun 10 a.m.–6 p.m, admission free

[web.rgzm.de/museen/museum-fuer-antike-schiffahrt-mainz]

below left: Museum für antike Schiffahrt, No. 2 B Neutorstrasse

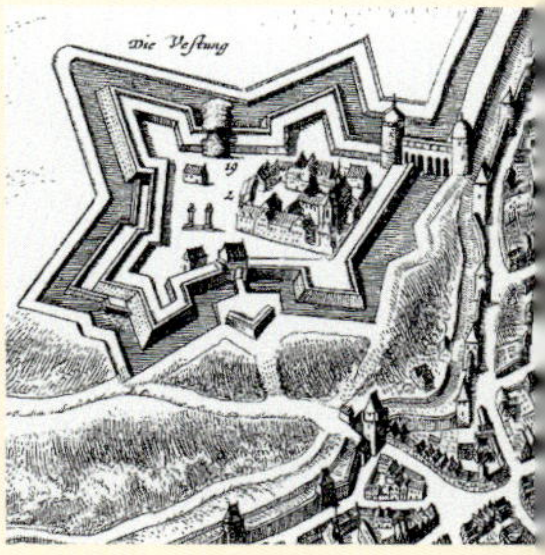

above: The citadel, copperplate engraving c. 1696, detail

left and above left: Citadel, commander's building, 1696

below: Corner bastion of the citadel, 1659–61

Citadel, Drusus stone, 9 AD., today's condition (right) and reconstruction (above)

above: Remnants of the Roman Gate

Gautor, 1670

below left: Alexanderturm (Alexander tower), Roman and c. 1500
below right: Haus Kupferberg, 1856 and 1860

an Pfaff around 1785 for the cathedral deanery, which collapsed in 1793. Also in 1793, all but two buildings of the Benedictine monastery on the northwest half of the site were destroyed. These were used as 'Benedictine barracks' until they were finally pulled down in 1912. There was a barracks housed within the citadel until 1918, and thereafter an educational establishment. Today, it houses civic administration offices and schools.
The 'Drususstein' (Drusus Stone) stands in the middle of the citadel grounds. It is the remains of a cenotaph that was once 30m high, erected by Roman legionaries in 9 AD in honour of their fallen commander Drusus. Also called the 'Eichelstein' (Acorn Stone) due to its shape and later used as a watchtower, it used to stand beside the road connecting the camp on 'Kästrich' hill with the one in Weisenau.

Römertor (Roman Gate)

Three metres below street level on Kästrich hill remnants remain preserved of the late Roman city gate dating from 360–70, which was rebuilt after the legionaries' camp was abandoned. It once rose up over the camp's via praetoria, laid in the 1st century and on which chariot tracks are still visible.

Kupferberg Museum

No. 17–19 Kupferbergterrasse

In 1847 Christian Adalbert Kupferberg (1824–76) from Mainz founded his champagne cellars in Neustadt an der Haardt (along the wine route) and settled in Mainz in 1850. Kupferberg purchased parts of the cellars of the nearby Altmünsterkloster (Monastery "Altmünster") and extended them. Today there are more than 60 vaulted cellars on seven storeys providing a consistant climate. Worth a visit is the building complex constructed in 1856 which hosts an exhibition about wine. Especially worth seeing is the so-called "Traubensaal" (Grape Hall), an art nouveau room which has been exhibited in the German pavilion during the world exhibition in Paris in 1900.
(Tel. 06131/9230)

St. Stephan (St. Stephen's)

From 975–992, Archbishop Willigis (975–1011) had a collegiate chapter house built to serve him as a last resting place. The current building was built on the Ottonian foundations from 1290–1338. It is now the oldest cross-shaped, double chancel hall church in the central Rhine district. Many of the 600 benefactors were buried in the cloister, probably built by the stonemason Valentinus and completed in 1499. There are numerous gravestones and coats of arms in their memory. Up as far as the frieze on the ogival arch, the tower is likely to still be from Willigis's time. In the 16th century, a guardroom was built into it, which was still lived in until 1911. In 1740, the tower was given a Baroque cap, which was reconstructed in 1962. Since secularisation in 1802, St. Stephen's has been a parish church. The second largest sacral building in Mainz, the church was damaged in 1857 by an explosion in the nearby magazine and was destroyed to its foundations in the Second World War. Reconstruction of the church was completed in 1962, that of the cloister in 1970.

The church's high quality interior furnishings include a Gothic block altar dating from the 13th century, rediscovered in 1947 and now used as the main altar; the wing altar with a crucifixion scene of historical artistic importance as the central panel (c. 1410); the late Gothic figures of God the Father Enthroned and 'Anna Selbtritt' (both c. 1500); the font dating from 1330; and the Sacrament Shrine dating from 1500 with stone figures from the same period on the side of Saint Stephen and Mary Magdalena. The iconic gravestone for Count Gottfried IX von Eppstein-Münzenberg (d. 1522, below the tower to the left) is the former ledger stone of a tomb.

St. Stephen's is visited today predominantly because of its nine church windows created by Marc Chagall. Vicar Klaus Mayer met the Jewish artist in 1973 and was ultimately able to engage him for this project, even though Chagall had never visited Mainz. St. Stephen's remains the only church in Germany for which Chagall ever did any work. The then 91 year old artist's first window for the church was installed in 1978, and he completed the last shortly before his death in 1985. Themes from the Old and New Testaments are juxtaposed in the six windows of the east chancel and the three of the transept as a

St. Stephen, sepulchral monument for Gottfried von Diez († 1522)

St. Stephen's, 14th century, west choir and crossing tower

St. Stephen, former chapter room, 15th century, Strohut epitaph, 1485 (above left) and cloister, 1462–99 (above right).

St. Stephen, church with cloister seen from the southwest.

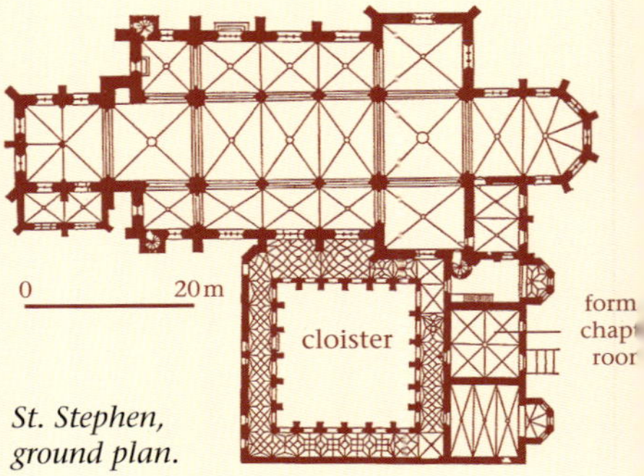

St. Stephen, ground plan.

symbol of Jewish-Christian solidarity and international understanding. The far simpler windows in the side aisles and baptism chapel are merely intended to serve as lead into the actual main works. They were created by Charles Marq, head of the Jacques Simon glass studios in Reims, with whom Chagall worked for 28 years.

To the south, this parish church is adjoined by the cloister (1462–92), the most significant from the Late Gothic era in Rhineland Palatinate. A keystone names the stonemason Valentinus as the builder. The cloister is 24 x 24 metres in size and surprises visitors above all through its original reticulated vaulting with star-shaped ribbed figures and through its keystones and corbels, filled with coats of arms relating to its benefactors. Epitaphs and gravestones indicate that the cloister used to serve as the last resting place for those connected with the chapter. Canon Hermann Strohut and his brother Arnold's crucifixion relief, donated in 1485, and the little Mount of Olives (c. 1490), are worthy of note. To the east the church is adjoined by two chapels and a hall passage with a central column (probably the former chapter room).

right: St. Stephen, windows of the east choir by Marc Chagall, 1978–85.

Older Dalberg House, No. 1 Ballplatz, donjon, middle of the 14th century. In the background the tower of the Chapel of the Magi can be seen, 1860–61

Ballplatz (Ball Square)

The name 'Ballplatz' harks back to a wooden theatre mentioned in 1760. To the west, the square is bordered by two nobles' houses from the Renaissance period; to the east by the Court of the Electors of Cologne, which, with the exception of the area around the gate, was pulled down and reconstructed in 1976–77; and, to the north by a diagonal building from the 1970's. The bronze 'Määnzer Mädchen' (Mainz Maidens) fountain was made by the Salzburg sculptor Magnus in 1978.

The 'Älterer Dalberger Hof' (Older Dalberg House) at no. 1 Ballplatz links back to the residential tower of the Königstein-Eppstein nobles, which dates from the middle of the 14th century. Dalberg commissioned the site to be enhanced in 1598, by adding extensions such as corner oriels. In the second half of the 18th century, the building was also given a mezzanine floor. There is a Madonna dating from 1677 above the border of the portal, which itself dates from 1710. The Madonna was created to mark the 200th anniversary of Mainz University and adorns the university seal to this day. The 18th century Baroque stairwell has a wrought-iron balustrade with a double crest of the Eltz-Dalberg family.

above right:
Fountain „Määnzer Mädchen", 1978, and Fechenbach House, No. 3 Ballplatz, beginning of the 18th century and 1951

above and right:
Older Dalberg House, No. 1 Ballplatz, 1598, portal from 1710

In 1846, the 'English Ladies' (Maria Ward Sisters) acquired the site's garden. In 1860–61 the New Romanesque 'Dreikönigskapelle' (Chapel of the Magi) was built in the gardens to plans by Ludwig Metternich, the Grand Duchy's district planning officer, and in 1880 a school house was built (enlarged in 1894 and made higher in 1898).

The 'Fechenbacher Hof' (Fechenbach House) at no. 3 Ballplatz was built at the start of the 18th century for the barons of Fechenbach. As in the Älteren Dalberger Hof, the Maria Ward School also held lessons in this house. Gutted by fire in 1945, the building was reconstructed in 1951.

Gutenberg Square, Staatstheater, 1829–33 and 1910–12

Gutenbergplatz (Gutenberg Square)

Gutenberg Square was laid out at the expense of a number of existing civic structures as the main component of the 'Rue Napoleon' (later 'Ludwigstrasse'), a major new road axis ordered by Napoleon in 1804. Initial construction was to plans by Eustache Saint-Far (1746–1828) and then, from 1819, by Augustin Wetter in collaboration with Georg Moller. Reconstruction after World War II followed designs by Ernst May.
The square is named after the monument to Gutenberg, erected in 1837 to honour the 'city's greatest son'. The monument was made by Berthel Thorvaldsen in Rome in 1832–3 and cast in bronze in the Crozatier workshop in Paris in 1836. It shows Gutenberg holding the printing types in his right hand and the Bible in his left. Attached to the plinth are two bronze reliefs, also made by Thorvaldsen.
Instead of a 'comedy playhouse' ordered by Napoleon in 1804 (foundation stone laid 1808), a 'Stadttheater' (city theatre, since 1989 'Staatstheater') was built in 1829–33 to plans by Georg Moller (1784–1852), the senior building officer of the Grand Duchy of Hessen. City building officer Adolf Gelius extended the semi-circle of the auditorium in 1910–12 by adding a foyer similar to that in the Semper Opera House in Dresden. The side reliefs, tragedy on the left, comedy on the right, were created by the sculptor Ludwig Lipp in 1910.

Schillerplatz (Schiller Square)

Schillerplatz is one of the grandest squares in the city. It is surrounded by the most stately of Mainz's noble houses from the Baroque era and leads into the Schillerstrasse, which is lined with equally impressive buildings. The trees are laid out as they were in 1768, as is the positioning of the carnival fountain, on the spot of a former running well.
The bronze carnival fountain was made by Blasius Spreng and erected in

Monument to Gutenberg on Gutenberg Square, 1832–33

Ostein House, No. 1 Schillerplatz, 1747–52.

below: Monument to Schiller on Schiller Square, 1862.

1967. It shows over 200 figures and symbols of the Mainz carnival and its interwoven history of high jinks, which are given added vitality by the fountain's rippling water.

The oval bowed 'Osteiner Hof' (Ostein House) sets the character of the square. It was designed between 1747–52 for the brother of Elector Friedrich Karl von Ostein (1743–63) by Johann Valentin Thomann (who also built St. Peter's Church) in collaboration with Anselm Franz von Ritter zu Grünstein. The rich Rococo interior was destroyed in the Second World War. Nevertheless, the spacious entrance hall and staircase still convey its former Baroque grandeur. Since Napoleonic times, the residence has served as a base for military authorities and thus today serves the German Army as a regional headquarters. Every year at eleven minutes past eleven on the eleventh day of the eleventh month the motto of the carnival campaign is proclaimed from the ballroom balcony.

There is a copy of the Virgin Mother from one of the 'Altenmünster' houses on the wall of the west wing in 'Gaustrasse' (the original is in the State Museum).

The western border of Schillerplatz incorporates the 'Bassenheimer Hof' (Bassenheim House), a noble residence built from 1750–55 by Anselm Franz von Ritter zu Grünstein for Countess von Bassenheim, the sister of Elector Friedrich Karl von Ostein. A coat of arms indicating the alliance between the Bassenheim-Waldbott family and the Ostein family appears on the Rococo ironwork of the first-floor balcony and with rocaille cartouches in the gabled area of the central wing. The crest shows a swan, as the heraldic animal of Bassenheim-Waldbotts, and a dog as that of the Osteins. Restored in 1947–48 after being badly damaged in the War, the three-storey building has housed the Rhineland Palatinate Ministry of Internal Affairs since 1960.

In 1859, the city fathers of Mainz decided to erect a monument to mark Friedrich von Schiller's 100th birthday. The standing figure and stone

plinth were cast in bronze in 1862 based on a model by Johann Baptist Scholl the Younger.

Schönborner Hof (Schönborn House)

(No. 11 Schillerstrasse)

Local civic administrator Philipp Erwein, brother of the ruling Elector Johann Philipp (1647–73), had this house built in 1668–70 according to plans by Clemens Hinck. After the fall of the Electorate shortly after 1800, the house became a barracks and the main building was raised. Following destruction in 1945, it has been restored to its former two-storey Baroque condition. The building acts today as a French cultural institute. Striking features include the scrollwork on the gables of the corner risalits, the greatly protruding balcony with swan neck gable pediments and the coat of arms of the Schönborn family.

Carnival fountain, 1967, and Bassenheim House, No. 3 Schillerplatz, 1750–55

below left: Schönborn House, No. 11 Schillerstrasse, 1668–70

below: Schiller Square with carnival fountain, Ostein House and Bassenheim House

below and above left: Provisions store, 1863–67

above right: Altmünsterkirche, after 1656, 1895 and 1958–60

Provisions Store

In 1863–67, a monumental, castle-like provisions store (no. 11A Schillerstrasse) was built on the former garden of the Schönborner Hof. This included a wartime bakery for the Prussian and Austrian garrison of the Federation fortifications in Mainz.

Professor's Houses, 1784–86

Professor's Houses

(Nos. 5, 7 & 9 Neue Universitätsstrasse)

By order of Elector Friedrich Karl Josef von Erthal, houses for Mainz University professors were built from 1784–86 between Erthaler Hof and 'Altmünsterkirche' on the site of the Altmünster monastery, which had been pulled down in 1781. Three houses remain of the nine classicist model homes built at that time to designs by the mathematics professor and engineering captain Rudolf Eickemeyer. The original half-timbered court buildings were pulled down only in 1972. Both Goethe and the Humboldts stayed at one time in the professor's houses, which rate as fine examples of middle-class domestic culture of the late 18th century.

Altmünsterkirche (Oldminster Church)

(No. 25 Münsterstrasse)

The Altmünster monastery was probably established by the holy Benedictine abbess Bilhildis around 700. In 1235, it passed into the ownership of the Cistercians. In 1656, the monastery building had to give way to construction of the bastion complex and was rebuilt 100 metres away. After the dissolution of the monastery in 1781, the building was used for a while as a protestant church (1802–08), but predominantly as a military hospital. From 1918–30 a garrison church for the French occupation, the church building, adapted to the New Romanesque style in 1895, was taken over by the protestant church community. Destroyed in

1944, the building now has the modern architectural lines of 1958–60, based on plans by Otto Vogel of Trier.

Erthaler Hof (Erthal House)

(No. 44 Schillerstrasse)

The regional administrative offices for the Mainz and Bingen area are housed in this grand Baroque residence of 1734–41, constructed for his family with an impressive courtyard frontage by the gentleman architect and Privy Councillor Philipp Christoph Freiherr von und zu Erthal. Having survived the War, the building is the only aristocratic residence in Mainz still with its original roof construction. A coat of arms symbolising the alliance between the Erthal and Bettendorf families appears within the gable on the streetside façade. On the extension to the right there is a sculpture of Saint Bilhildis, the founder of the Altmünster monastery. The stairwell has also been preserved, with a spacious staircase and stucco ceilings.

Erthal House, No. 44 Schillerstrasse, 1734–41

St. Emmeran's

(No. 19 Emmeranstrasse)

Today used as a community centre, this former parish church was consecrated to the holy Bishop Emmeran († 625) of Regensburg. The oldest part

below: St. Emmeran, choir vault (left) and view from north east

St. Emmeran, choir vault, c. 1300

above right: Armklarakirche, c. 1331

Stadion House, No. 15 Große Bleiche, 1728–33 und 1949

of the building is a five-storey Romanesque tower dating from the end of the 12th century. When the subsequent Gothic church, a three-aisled basilica, was built around 1300, the tower was integrated into the new building. The church suffered severe war damage in 1945, and in the course of the reconstruction work in 1966, the tower superstructure was removed in favour of today's pyramid roof.

Armklarakirche (Poor Clares Church)

(No. 8 Adolf-Kolping-Strasse)

In 1331, a woman named Mechthildis founded this church, consecrated to St. Antonius, which was extended by the addition of a monastery in the same year. Having previously been deconsecrated, the sacral building was acquired in 1620 by the 'Armen Klarissen' (Poor Clares), who enhanced it in 1625 by installing the nuns' chancel and again at the start of the 18th century with several monastery buildings. From 1802 until its destruction in 1942, many educational organisations were housed there. Gutted by fire in 1942, and today used as the chapel for the Kolping House, the church was rebuilt in 1948, the monastery buildings pulled down and replaced in 1966 by a new building that houses the Bischöfliches Institut für Kirchenmusik (Episcopal Institute for Church Music). In the chancel is the only preserved Gothic tableaux (c. 1350) of any of the churches in Mainz. When the church was rebuilt, the monastery portal (1724–27), with the figure of Saint Clare created by von Burkardt in 1725, was reused in its old position.

Stadioner Hof

(No 15 Große Bleiche)

This stately Baroque building dating from 1728–33 stands on main street of the Baroque 'Bleichviertel' (Bleaching Quarter), the 'Große Bleiche'. Anselm Franz von Ritter zu Grünstein (1692–1765) provided the design for Lothar Friedrich von Rollingen. After the latter's death in 1737, it was acquired by Friedrich Graf von Stadion-Thannhausen and his wife Anna Maria von Sickingen. In 1756, the mother of the romantic poets Clemens and Bettina Brentano was born here. The building was damaged during war and reconstructed in 1949.

Neuer Brunnen (New Fountain)

In 1726, to provide a better water supply to the 'bleaching quarter', 'Bleichviertel', Elector Lothar Franz von Schönborn had a draw well installed, the first water pipeline in the city. The obelisk is adorned with ornaments (symbols of the arts, sciences and crafts). The allegorical figures of Rhine and Main, designed in 1726 by court sculptor Franz M. Hiernle (copy dates from 1877), were complemented in 1828 by two sphinx-like lions by Joseph Scholl.

Jüngerer Dalberger Hof (Newer Dalberg House)

(No. 4 Klarastrasse)

above left and right: Newer Dalberg House, No. 4 Klarastrasse, 1715–18

Planned back in 1707, this generously dimensioned family home for the barons of Dalberg with its magnificent façade was built by the master stonemason, Caspar Herwartel (1675–1720), on the site of several older houses. Gutted by fire as a result of the artillery bombardment of Mainz in 1793, this palatial residence was rebuilt in 1828–29 by Paul Arnold, director of building, as a palace of justice for the Grand Duchy (now the 'Peter Cornelius Konservatorium', a music academy).

left: New Fountain, 1726, 1828 and 1877

Old University, 1615–18, and St. Quintin, 1288–1330

St. Quintin's Church, 1288–1330, upper storey of the tower from 1489

Of the neighbouring Baroque buildings that surrounded the inner courtyard, the library building to the south has survived (built c. 1722, added to in 1891). The north wing, the detention house from 1831–34, replaced the Baroque outbuildings and stables.

Alte Universität (Old University)

(No. 17 Alte Universitätsstrasse)

Resident since 1577 in the Franciscan monastery situated opposite, the Jesuits built a lecture building for the university in 1615–18, inscribing both of its Renaissance portals with the words 'Domus Universitatis'. Created by Johann Jacob Juncker, the coats of arms of the Mainz cathedral chapter and Elector Johann Schweickhardt von Kronberg also appear in the triangular gables. The building was used from 1792 as a barracks and from 1889 as a schoolhouse and civic offices. After the fire of 1942, it was rebuilt in 1951–52 as a cubic, institute building. One of the roof turrets destroyed in 1793 was reconstructed above the centre of the building in 1952. A memorial plate refers to Johannes Gutenberg, whose last resting place was in the Franciscan church, which was pulled down in 1742.

St. Quintin's Church

(Quintinsstrasse 1)

St. Quintin's, first mentioned in 744, is the oldest parish church in Mainz. It was built between 1288–1330 and extended in 1489 with the addition of a tower, upper floor and living quarters. The square layout of the three-aisled nave is similar to that of the now no longer existing Liebfrauenkirche (Church of our Lady). The original church furnishings were nearly all lost

in the Second World War. In contrast to the Baroque tower cap, it was possible to reconstruct the pillared baldachin above the high altar built in 1739 according to designs by Maximilian von Welsch. There is also a former altarpiece inside the church showing the Ascension of Mary by Franz Anton Maulbertsch (1724–96).

St. Christoph

(Christofsstrasse 8)

First mentioned as a chapel in 839, this is the church in which Gutenberg was baptised. Its oldest part is the Late Romanesque north tower, dating from before 1240 and increased in height in the 14th/15th century. The nave dates

St. Quintin, 1288–1330, Baroque interior

above left and centre: St. Christoph, tower before 1240, raised in the 14th/15th century, nave 1280–1330

above right: St. Joseph's chapel, 1715–24

Knebelscher Hof, 1588–98 and 1953–55, with original Renaissance oriel

from 1280–1330 and was remodelled in Baroque times. The building, including the apse built in 1761, was destroyed in 1945. Only the perimeter walls remained. The church was left as a ruin as a memorial to the dead of World War II. The frieze created by Heinz Hemrich in 1962 between the concrete supports of the north side aisle depicts both pleading and destructive looking hands.

Josefskapelle St. Joseph's chapel

(No. 4 Hintere Christofgasse)

Next to Christopher's is the Josefskapelle, a remnant of the Jesuit novitiate built in 1701–19.– The octagonal building, originally built in 1715–18 to designs by the city's master builder Johannes Weydt, with a library floor added in 1723–24, was reconstructed after its destruction in 1942.– Above the grand pillared portal is a figure of Saint Joseph, created by Burkhard Zamels in 1720.

Next to the chapel stands the "Knebelsche Hof" (No. 2 Hintere Christofsgasse). The three-storey Renaissance building was constructed in 1588–98.

Karmeliterkirche Carmelite Church

(No. 5 Karmeliterplatz)

Active in Mainz since 1270, the Carmelites built this towerless monastery church between 1326–1404 as a typical mendicant order church. Used in the intervening years as a magazine, the church, newly consecrated to the Ascension of Mary, was taken over in 1924 by Dutch Carmelite fathers. Particular features of the church include the original murals in the sacristy, the heavily restored vaulted paintings in the chancel (15th century) and the Carmelite Madonna (c. 1400). In 1802, the associated monastery, built from 1700–13, was secularised and deconsecrated. In 1907, it was converted into a school according to plans by city planning officer Adolf Gelius, retaining the four-wing layout.

Former Dienheimer Hof

(Corner of Mitternachtsgasse and Bauerngasse)

Constructed in 1623–25, the triangular courtyard complex of the former Dienheimer Hof with its polygon staircase tower is adorned by a typical Renaissance gable with splendid scrollwork.

Carmelite Church, 1326–1404: Choir vault (above left), exterior (above right) and Pietà, early 15th century (below left)

below right: Dienheimer Hof, 1623–25

Natural History Museum, entrance building and giant sand clock

Natural History Museum, primeval horse (above), skeleton (below left) und Quagga group (below centre)

Natural History Museum

(Mitternacht/Reichklarastrasse 10)

The museum is housed in the Reichklarakloster (Rich Clares monastery), founded in 1272 by the Clare Franciscan sisters and dissolved in 1781. During use as a military bakery from 1793–1899, the church served as a magazine and flour store. In 1906, Adolf Gelius and Friedrich Pützer converted the monastery buildings into the natural history museum. Parts of the buildings were lost between 1831 and 1902, and they also suffered war damage in 1942. Nevertheless, large sections of the typical mendicant order church (c. 1300), featuring a double-aisled design, are retained. These include a cross-shaped hall that originally supported the nun's gallery. Today, the museum entrance is in the modern, glass 'Turm der Zeiten' (Tower of Ages), in which Wiesbaden artist Hieronymous Perret's painting interprets themes of linking time and the history of creation. In front of the door is the most accurate 'Riesensanduhr' (giant sand clock) in the world.

The museum, the largest and most important natural history museum in Rhineland Palatinate, has displays of regional rocks and minerals, fossilised discoveries and preserved animals and plants. The museum's treasures include a Tasmanian marsupial wolf, a Java rhinoceros and the world famous Quagga group.

Natural History Museum, former Clare Franciscan convent, around 1300, former monastery church (above) and vault below the former nun's gallery (below).

Natural History Museum:
open:
Tue 10 a.m.–8 p.m.,
Wed 10 a.m.–2 p.m.
Thu–Sun 10 a.m.–5 p.m.

Deutschhausplatz

The Deutschhausplatz, in front of the 'Deutschordenskommende' (The Commandery of the Order of the Teutonic Knights) on the city side, opens into 'Große Bleiche' and is bordered to the west by St. Peter's and to the south by the old 'Zeughaus' (armoury).

The Deutschhaus (Teutonic House) at no. 12 Deutschhausplatz is an impressive Baroque building dating from 1730–40. It has a stately central wing and a courtyard of honour enclosed by two free-standing pavilions and a courtyard fence adorned with ornate figures. The High Grand Master of the Teutonic Order, simultaneously Elector and Archbishop Franz Ludwig

Teutonic House, No. 12 Deutschhausplatz, main building dates from 1730–40

Pavilions and courtyard fence of the Deutschhaus

New Armoury, 1738–40

Pfalzgraf Fürst von Neuenburg (1729–32), had the complex built by the architect Anselm Franz Freiherr von Ritter zu Grünstein (1692–1765) as a new headquarters building for the Order. The Rhenish-German National Convention was constituted here in 1793, the first democratic German parliament. From 1804–13 the building served as accommodation for Napoleon, and from 1819–1918 it was a residence of the Grand Duchy. After being badly damaged in the War, it was rebuilt in 1950–53 as the seat of the Rhineland Palatinate State Parliament. The Deutschhaus was originally surrounded by numerous other Baroque buildings including St. Gangolf's Church.

The 'Neue Zeughaus' (New Armoury), dating from 1738–40, was built in equally magnificent style and similar

Old Armoury, 1604–05, No. 8 Deutschhausplatz

above and left:
Electoral Palace, Römisch-Germanisches Zentralmuseum, 1628–1752

Römisch-Germanisches Zentralmuseum
opening hours:
Tue–Sun 10 a.m.–6 p.m.
Admission free
[web.rgzm.de/museen/roemisch-germanisches-zentralmuseum-mainz]

proportions and stands directly next to the Deutschhaus to the south. The design was provided by Maximilian Welsch for Elector Philipp Carl zu Eltz, whose crest of lions can be seen in the gable. The ornate figures on the exterior indicate the military character of the building as a magazine for the Electoral army. Today, the building is the State Chancellery and official residence of the Prime Minister of Rhineland Palatinate.
The Old Armoury (Altes Zeughaus) at no. 8 Deutschhausplatz was built in 1604–05. The coat of arms of the Elector of the time, Johann Adam von Bicken (1601–04), can be seen over the archway leading to the cellar. The building served as a store for military equipment, and from 1770 as a mint.

Electoral Palace and Römisch-Germanisches Zentralmuseum

(No. 2 Ernst-Ludwig-Platz)

Construction of the Electoral Palace began in 1628. The plan was for a 75-metre long wing extension on the side of the Rhine to connect the Martinsburg castle built in 1478–81 with the neighbouring 'Kanzleigebäude' (Chancellery building) to the south, dating from 1555–57, and the Gangolfskirche of 1570–81 (St. Gangolf's Church). Building took a long time and needed five different builders. In 1752, under Elector Friedrich Karl Graf von Ostein (1743–63) and his architect Anselm Franz Ritter von Grünstein, the 85m north wing and thus the whole angular

Römisch-Germanisches Zentralmuseum, statue of Jupiter, Italy, 1st century AD, copy

Römisch-Germanisches Zentralmuseum, egyptian relief (above), late celtic top part of a standard in the shape of a wild boar, small ivory box, 4th century, and goblet of Tassilo, c. 780, copies (below)

complex was finally finished. What arose was a magnificent, three-floor showcase building, the original red paintwork of which has now been restored.
The striking complex of palace, moated castle, chancellery building and palace chapel only survived until the French occupation under Napoleon. Except for the palace, which was put to different uses from 1797 as barracks, a military hospital and customs magazine, all of the other buildings mentioned were torn down in 1807 or 1814. However, Eustache Saint-Far (1746– 1828) added to the angular palace building in 1807 with a single-storey east wing, the so-called 'Steinhalle' (stone hall), formerly a customs hall.
It was not until 1842 that the palace was given a meaningful use as town library, art gallery, ancient history museum and Römisch-Germanisches Zentralmuseum. In 1942, the building was gutted by fire and its important interior fittings destroyed. Today, the Rhine wing and 'stone hall' are used as the Römisch-Germanisches Zentralmuseum, while the north wing is utilised for conferences, concerts, balls and carnival events. The remains of the foundations of Martinsburg castle, destroyed in 1807, can be seen in the lawns in front of the complex.

Römisch-Germanisches Zentralmuseum

Affiliated with the astonishingly wide-ranging collection of the Römisch-Germanisches Zentralmuseum, established in 1852, are a number of other organisations. These include restoration and reproduction workshops involved in work such as conserving the iceman of South Tirol and restoring Peruvian discoveries from a prince's grave.
Originals and top quality reproductions from the museum's workshops are displayed in bright exhibition rooms. Prehistoric cultural development from the early bronze age to the Germanic era is clearly explained in the 'stone hall' with exhibits from all over the world (e.g. finds from Troy, ritual 'Kultwagen' sculpture, Greek and Italian ceramics, the 'Goldkegel' (gold cone) of Ezelsdorf-Buchgold and other gold finds). The Roman section on the first floor of the Rhine wing shows reliefs, ceramics, glass, military equipment, sarcophagi and more. The early middle ages on the second floor deals with every aspect of the Franconian era up to Charlemagne.

above: first exhibition room of the late antique and early medieval section. Table top with hen and chickens belonging to the treasure of the Langobard Queen Theodelinde (589– 626), copy.

St. Peter, 1749–56, façade (above left) and pulpit in the style of Rococo

St. Peter's

(No. 2 Petersstrasse)

The Rococo St. Peter's Church, made quite striking by its twin-tower façade, was built between 1749–56 to plans by Johann Valentin Thomann (1695–1777) in place of the Marienkirche (St. Mary's Church) established by Archbishop Friedrich von Lothringen in 944. After being totally gutted by fire in 1945, comprehen-

sive reconstruction work began four years later.
Today the three-aisled, splendidly designed interior can once again be experienced as a 'theatrum sacrum', i.e. a Baroque inspired theatre of architecture, painting, sculpture and stucco presented as an holistic creation of space. The wooden pulpit was created by Johann Förster with busts by Peter Heinrich Hencke. The free-standing baldachin altar in the chancel dates from 1762. The north side altar is dominated by a crucifix by Hans Backoffen from the early 16th century. The magnificent ceiling mural shows portrayals from the life of the Apostle Peter. It was originally created by the famous Joseph Ignaz Appiani from 1752–55 and restored / reconstructed after being destroyed in the War by the painter Karl Manninger and his pupil Hermenegild Peiker between 1979–89 based on black and white templates. The modern bronze celebratory altar was made by Gernot Rumpf in 1989. The organ dates from 1954 and comes from the Carmelite church in Njmwegen.

St. Peter, 1749–56, view into the choir (right) and ceiling fresco (below)

Landesmuseum Mainz, 1766–70

Landesmuseum Mainz (State Museum)

(No. 49–51 Große Bleiche)

Landesmuseum Mainz opening hours:
Tue 10 a.m.– 8 p.m.
Wed–Sun 10 a.m.– 5 p.m.

www.landesmuseum-mainz.de

The Mainz State Museum is housed in the former 'Golden Steed Barracks' that was part of the Electoral stables built in 1766–67 and designed by the Electoral director of building Jakob Joseph Schneider. The name stems from a gilded jumping horse used to accentuate the gable. By 1770, the building was extended into a four-winged complex by the addition of a riding hall and a further wing. Once cavalry barracks, the Ancient History Museum was set up here in 1937, which after being destroyed in the War was rebuilt in 1950–61 as the State Museum.

The art collection, the most significant in the State of Rhineland Palatinate, was based initially on regional art and a gift of Napoleon's from the year 1803. The museum is now considered to be one of the oldest in Germany and shows a broad spectrum of European art and crafts (e.g. the Akeleipokal, or 'Aquilegia Cup', Rhenish stoneware and tapestries) from many eras, including: prehistoric beginnings (e.g. gold jewellery from the early bronze age and ornate Celtic disks); Roman times (e.g. stone monuments in the 'Steinhalle' stone hall, Jupiter

Landesmuseum Mainz, stone hall with stone monuments from Roman times (above), Art Nouveau vase, c. 1895–1900 (below left), helmet from the first quarter of the 6th century (below right)

column, Dionysos bottle and ceramic vessels): the early Middle Ages (e.g. golden almadin buckle, claw beaker and filigree clasps); the Middle Ages (e.g. the Dietrichstein stone, Bretzenheim Madonna and panel painting); the Renaissance and Baroque eras (e.g. paintings by Jordaens, van Honthorst, van Ruysdael, Lorrain and Tiepolo); and up to the present (e.g. works by Polke, Klinger, Corinth, Lehmbruck, Picasso and Rothko). As well as the State's largest graphical collection the museum also has a wide variety of Art Nouveau glass (e.g. Tiffany, Gallé, Daum Frères and Nancy), porcelain from Hoechst and Judaica (e.g. Thoraschild and Thorarolle). Other treasures in the museum include Germany's largest Tàpies collection, which has been integrated into the 20th century section. The rich wealth of permanent exhibits is complemented by special exhibitions, educational museum events and lectures.

Dativius Victor Arch (near the Electoral Palace), 3rd century AD, reconstruction. The arch frieze shows the signs of the zodiac

Christuskirche
(Kaiserstr. 56)

In 1886, the City of Mainz gave the protestant community established in 1802 a plot of building land, on which the Christuskirche was built between 1897–1903 according to plans by the city master builder Eduard Kreyßig in the Neorenaissance style. After his death, construction was completed by the Swedish architekt Franz Fredriksson in an amended, simplified form. After being damaged in the War in 1945, it was restored in 1952 under the direction of Otto Vogel, with the interior given a simpler appearance. With its towering dome, the central structure makes the same striking impression in the new town as the cathedral does in the old.

REGISTER